BOSS UP YOUR THOUGHTS!

ATTITUDES AND AFFIRMATIONS FOR CONFIDENCE, POSITIVE THINKING & BEING YOUR BEST SELF

RÉGINA HARRIS

CONTENTS

Dedicated to the memory of
Betty Harris and Eleanor Hart
You are missed one-thousand times over.

FOREWORD

From the day we first met almost 12 years ago, I knew immediately by her presence, I had met a woman I would never forget. RéGina was intelligent, assertive, and proving herself a force to be reckoned with!

Over the years, I've come to understand that special women like her are not necessarily advantaged or from privileged backgrounds. Instead, they are women who have risen above some of life's most difficult challenges and circumstances. Initially, as a co-worker to becoming a mentor and good friend, I have had the privilege of seeing RéGina continue to transform and impact other people and organizations around her.

I have witnessed RéGina soar as a single mother raising twins, finding love at fifty, and bettering herself tirelessly with continual education and personal advancement. All while setting a stellar example of a person with ethics and integrity.

RéGina's consistency and positive attitude are what sets her apart from her peers. Her constant support and willingness to share have helped me get through some of the toughest challenges of my personal and professional life. I am forever grateful to call her my sister-friend and excited she is continuing her outreach through this body of work.

- Kimberly Marie

ACKNOWLEDGEMENTS

Thank you to my sister-friends who listened when I needed to talk or bounce around countless ideas. You checked-in on me regularly and held me accountable even when I was off schedule. You ensured I enjoyed adequate downtime with pitchers of mimosas or bottles of wine, recharged, and then got back to business.

Much respect and love to my Las Vegas family; your diva wisdom has been invaluable and appreciated.

Last but surely not least, thank you to my incredibly thoughtful and supportive husband for affording me the freedom to pursue whatever my heart desires.

I love you, and I am grateful that you are part of my life.

PREFACE

It can be hard being out here trying to do you. Stress, craziness, heartache, disappointment, and a whole bunch of other nonsense have a way of sneaking up on you without warning and bringing with it all sorts of thoughts and feelings. There's no question about how much these perceptions play into how we see ourselves.

And anything unchecked or allowed to continue unevaluated is subject to become a liability, including our thoughts. It's essential to balance our thinking if we want to stay on point. Feeding the mind with positive interpretations will motivate us to see what is possible mentally before being in a position to make it happen. We need encouragement, reassurance, and inspiration to build resilience and counter the self-bullying that creeps into our thoughts without permission. And sometimes, we just need to be reminded about truths we already know but may have chosen to ignore.

This book is a collection of amazingly powerful words written to inspire and affirm positive self-perceptions while motivating you to make a few self-adjustments. There's nothing wrong with upgrading your thoughts, updating your attitude, re-evaluating connections, and retiring anything (or anyone) from your life that isn't positive or productive. A little mental house cleaning goes a long way towards improving your life for the better, and you'll be happier.

We are what we think we are, and we get only those things we believe we deserve, so boss up your thoughts and upgrade your life!

- RéGina

Expressions

*B*eautiful is not a thing; it's a feeling, a self-perception. Mirrors reflect only what we choose to see. Men may comment on what they see, but their words don't make us beautiful. Beauty radiates from within.

You are attractive because of your essence, who you are, and how you treat people. Genuinely caring and helping, never looking for accolades, social attention, or favors in return.

We see your humble heart and honest intentions through your forgiveness and love and choosing relationships and family over materials or money. Hair, makeup, and nails are not your prerequisites for beauty.

Inner beauty is something words can't tear down. Its glow can't be dimmed. Use each day to showcase your heart, and the world will see beauty at its best.

જે જે

I am beautiful inside and out.

LOVIN' MY FLAWS

*L*ife isn't about being flawless; it's about being unpretentious and genuine regardless of what that looks like. It's about being comfortable with who you are and all your quirky ways.

Be prideful and unapologetic about your imperfections. Others may see them as blemishes or shortcomings. They are far from it. These are the distinct aesthetic qualities that make you different from everyone else.

When you strive for perfection, you hide your true self. You exert all your efforts trying to please other people and live up to their idea of how you should look or act. You no longer see authenticity as good enough. Instead, perfection becomes a priority for everything. Perfectionism is exhausting, expensive, and will either drive you to drink or right into a straitjacket.

Stop trying to make yourself into someone you are not. It's ok to be different, so get good with it. The more you embrace who you are, the greater your confidence and success. There is nothing more stunning than a confident woman; it's attractive, alluring, and captivating. Don't let perfection become the enemy and get in your way.

Now go out and be stunning!

❧❧

The world can use a lot more of who you already are.

As women, mothers, wives, partners, caregivers, and professionals, we spend much of our time taking care of others. We have become warriors in the quiet, taking little or no time to care for ourselves. Exhausted warriors need to recharge their batteries. It's time to take your needs off the back burner and start putting yourself first. It is not selfish to protect your well-being. One life is all you have, and you must take care of it.

Our daily lives are constantly subjected to demands and expectations from others. Your spirit needs time to rejuvenate. Find time to practice daily acts of betterment and self-care. Celebrate every win, no matter how insignificant it may seem. Gift yourself with compliments and tokens of affection. Make small and consistent improvements to be better than you were the day before. You are deserving of the same things you unselfishly give to those you love, don't shortchange yourself.

A restorative soul leads to a clear mind, and a clear mind enables you to make better decisions. Nurturing your spirit raises your self-esteem, increases your value, allows you to be more generous, and creates a fully experienced life.

ര❧ര❧

I deserve to be pampered and cared for.

GOD'S PLAN

*I*magine how much you could accomplish in life if you doubted your fears instead of doubting your dreams?

Everything God has for you is within your reach. His blueprint, however, is never without challenges. There are no promises of an easy ride. Jesus didn't have it easy, and he was the son of God, so we shouldn't expect his plan for us to be flawless. There will be bumps in the road. Be that as it may, nothing is impossible if you embrace the source of your strength and believe in the power of your prayers.

God stretches and challenges you with purpose. He wants you to develop and grow so you can be an inspiration for others. Do you trust that he has your back, has a plan, and is in control? Will you operate irrespective of fear and obstacles rather than run from them? Knowing where you stand is essential to living the divine life God has designed for you.

When you stop stressing and take things step-by-step, you can overcome what appears to be impossible. When you have faith in the process and stay the course, the rewards are great, and life is abundant.

ॐ ॐ

I am not worried.

MAKE ROOM FOR SERENDIPITY

*C*haos interferes with life all the time. When we give in to it, we become lost, confused, and sometimes broken. It is also the appropriate time for self-reflection and looking for the good in a bad situation.

Consequences are inherent in every action. Do not be discouraged. Continue moving forward, even amidst uncertainty. The end result isn't always bad, nor is it something we should fear, as fortune will typically favor the bold. Keep your mind ready, your spirit willing, and your eyes open.

When opportunity knocks, step out on faith, make the best choice possible, and do the damn thing!

જે જે

I ready for whatever, even if the end game is unclear.

Do not be afraid to be authentic. You were not shaped to imitate or duplicate anyone. Your look, tone, expressions, actions, and experiences make up your swag, a style unique only to you. Not everyone will like or agree with what you do, what you say, or what you represent.

People will always have something to say. Criticism and unsolicited opinions are a fact of life. How you choose to proceed paves the way for who you are today and who the world will see tomorrow. You can accept what they say, argue against it, or check it at the door and walk away. The less you say, the more peaceful your life will be.

Quality relationships are not a luxury; they are necessary, and spending time in a shitty one should never be an option. When people don't appreciate your presence, give them something they can't refuse...Your Absence!

ॐॐ

Respect and appreciation are non-negotiable.

NOT YOUR BEESWAX

The unhappiest people on the planet are the ones who care the most about what everyone else thinks. What other people think of you is not your problem and none of your business. When you concern yourself about the gossip someone else is spreading about you; you give them dominion over your life and health.

You allow their opinions to determine who you are or how far you will go. You start operating on someone else's agenda opening the door for them to derail you from the blessings, successes, and greatness you were working towards. Stay focus on your plan. You have no competition other than yourself. At the right time, the right people will take notice and see you seriously. Own your power. Protect it with a passion and use it for manifesting your dreams. You are the only one who can.

෨෨෨

My opinion is the one that counts most.

YOUR GIFT IS UNIQUENESS

*C*ommon, you? Absolutely not!

You are not ordinary, by no means.

Your uniqueness is a virtue.

It enables you to live your best life.

But, living your best life is tough if you are trying to be like other folks… typical and familiar.

God made you just right and good enough to be successful at the things you are trying to do. He DESIGNED you to be exclusive, phenomenal, and one of a kind. You are not supposed to be anyone else but yourself.

Stand out, live confidently in your authenticity and individuality regardless of how it is perceived.

෴

I am exactly right and good enough to be successful at the things I am trying to do.

TURN UP WHO YOU ARE

$\mathcal{I}$ am a fierce, soulful, gracefully talented woman who stands tall and speaks her mind.

I am passionate, independent, grounded, and important. I am bold, resilient, virtuous, and well-favored.

I am joyful and confident in what I know and the things I can do. I'm a lady with class, and no one can tell me any different.

I know my worth and bring value to the lives of the people around me.

I love boxing up the haters, living bold, loud, and celebrating life.

There will always be an audience somewhere appreciative of my realness, waiting on my ideas, and for me to step out and do something worthy of commentary.

Turning up who I am is my prerogative.

ॐ ॐ

Speak up loudly and often. You have a lot to offer and deserve to be seen.

CREATE YOUR JOURNEY

*T*here is nothing worse than being a slave to a life you absolutely despise while trying to "find yourself." No miracles are hanging out behind the couch, just waiting to reveal themselves and fix everything that's not to your liking. If you don't like the life you have, then create a new one. If you don't like the job you're working at, then get a new job. If you don't like the husband or man you have, then upgrade the model.

People and relationships come and go. Material things become old, worn out, and break, or we give them away. Money is earned, and it's spent. Control the things within your power to make your experiences meaningful. Envision what you want. Design situations that enable your beliefs, aspirations, ambitions, and talents to work together to bring your desires to fruition. You and only you have dominion over the encounters and events that shape your journey.

You know the impact you want to make. You know the person you want to be. You know the life you want to have. Go for it. Just go after it and don't look back unless it's somewhere you want to go back to.

ॐॐ

I am making room for my life to grow.

PERMISSION NOT NECESSARY

*Y*ou were made to live a copious and fruitful life.

You don't need permission to try and make the impossible a reality.

You don't need anyone's approval to unbox yourself.

God has placed within you everything you need to receive his blessings.

Ask for what you need and go after what you want.

Create whatever narrative you want for your life.

But be intentional with your decisions. Be deliberate in your actions. When your story becomes, your truth looking back will no longer be of interest to you.

❧❧

Life moves in one direction only, and I am moving with it.

here is it written that you must accept what you don't genuinely want, putting up with or enduring people and experiences that subtract from rather than adding to your life? Reading that crappy book instead of returning it. Ordering from the menu when nothing appeals to your taste buds instead of leaving. Staying in a non-loving relationship instead of saying this isn't for me and moving on.

Settling doesn't come from you; it takes from you everything you have to give and leaves you yearning, begging for something, anything to fill the void. When you settle, you give up all your rights to receive equal value and enjoy the same benefits from the other person. You will never have everything you want, or in the manner, you might want it. You do get to choose, and those choices should leave you feeling good and at peace with your decision.

As a child of God, his desire for us is to be filled with pursuing an abundant life, not wasting time accepting crap. You are entitled to enjoy this life because you only get one; that's it. There are no do-overs. Value the importance of living life on your terms. Stop settling for less than you deserve.

ॐ ॐ

When you raise your standards, people meet you where you are.

FORGIVE BUT NEVER FORGET

*here comes a time in life where the hurt we experience is so deep that we simply don't know what to do with it. We cuss, fuss, and maybe even act a fool, not once but many times over. It's unavoidable. Life hands out some hard knocks, and as long as you are here, there will always be another hurt around the corner just waiting for its turn. It knows forgiveness is not an easy thing to do.

We mistakenly think that forgiving someone means inviting them back into our lives, and they think the same. Your forgiveness isn't for them; it's for you. Forgiveness is allowing yourself to forget about those things that hurt. Let them go and drop um from your radar. It is about no longer feeling angry, spending time and energy trying to figure out how to extract some level of payback.

Forgiving breaks the person's hold over your emotions and prevents bitterness from blocking your joy and happiness. It lets you decide if you want to re establish your relationship and what type of contact you will have. Or, if you choose, you can retire them from your life because sometimes it's just best to keep someone an arm's length away or love them from afar.

Lessons learned the hard way makes us more inclined to forget them. Be that as it may, you should never forget what was taught. When you know better, you are supposed to do better. This is the value of being in the valley.

Favor and grace are necessary for healing, but the lessons from our experiences are essential for growth and maturity. Like falling dominoes, events, and decisions in our lives will generate a reaction.

What happens today is a result of what you do in the past. What happens in the future is the result of what you do today.

As difficult as it might be, what was taught should always be remembered, heeded, and applied.

৯৯

I am stronger today than I was yesterday.

NO REGRETS

Mistakes happen; it's inevitable. Life will kick your ass; that's bound to happen too. Don't regret any of it. Regrets stop you from pushing boundaries and attempting different things.

There is no value in wishing that you hadn't tried. When you're dead and gone, you get no more chances; instead, you will be left rolling around in the urn kicking up dust and pissed about the things you did not do.

When things don't work out, look over your shoulder, nod your head, make a new plan, and get back to it. Don't be afraid to make mistakes. Second chances are available to those of us who are willing to keep trying until we get it right.

‍ॐ‍ॐ

I appreciate all the experiences life brings to my doorstep.

STARTING OVER

*L*iving a blessed life requires you to be selective with who you share your time with.

We don't always get it right, though. We get caught up in meaningless friendships, forced interactions, or unnecessary conversations. A prosperous life cannot share the same space with stress and aggravation. Change becomes inevitable, and we find ourselves having to make new connections and let the old ones go.

Letting go and moving on to make room in life for the things and relationships that will genuinely add value is necessary if you want to live an abundant life. Sometimes starting over is easy, no drama, no headaches. Other times, you may just have to blow some shit up and burn the house down to get a clear view and find your way.

చొచ్

Do whatever you have to do to change your life and start doing things that make you happy.

*N*avigating the yellow brick road of daily life and achieving the outcomes you want for yourself is not easy. Seems like there are twists, turns, and unexpected events around almost every corner. More doors close than open, and people are quick to tell you about what you should or shouldn't do and why, rather than offer their support or help. But if you are dutiful, none of this will matter.

When you are committed to yourself, you move out of your comfort zone. Your focus is shielded from outside influences that do not support your agenda. Commitment shuts down the naysayers' voice, slaps disappointment in the face, and kicks uncertainty to the curb. It makes others uncomfortable, but it gives you the freedom to live life according to your definition of happiness and success.

৵৵

I am dedicated to doing what feels right for me.

*D*rama is a drop of real in a fake ass world designed to hijack your focus and deter you from the things you are working to achieve. When life is going good, and things are falling in your favor, drama always finds a way to make an appearance. Don't get caught up. There is no need to be in the midst of turmoil and confusion or take on the problems that come with it.

Participating in other people's drama is not your responsibility. When you see controversy and craziness starting to show up, turn your head, pick up your step, and move the hell on. It is not your place to understand or try and figure it out.

Engaging in nonsense is like having a dropped anchor tied to you; it will weigh you down and keep you from moving forward. Time spent is a currency that cannot be refunded. You got things to do, places to be, and less time in front of you than behind you to get there.

⁂

I do not put up with nonsense from people, especially those who don't matter.

YOUR INNER CIRCLE

*Y*ou should be able to count the number of people in your inner circle on one hand. I'm not saying you shouldn't be inclusive. You can be friendly, have umpteen many acquaintances, and address a million followers on Twitter or Instagram. But that's not a circle; that's an audience. Your inner circle is a small and exclusive club that is limited to people who have your best interest at heart. These are the people you can confide in and share your most intimate thoughts with. There is no worry of betrayal, ridicule, or judgment. They make you feel good, add positivity, and encourage you to achieve your goals.

What you put out into the universe and what you tolerate will attract people to you. Who walks into your life isn't something you can always control, but you can decide who makes the cut and stays. Be mindful and selective. You want a community of folks who will bring out the best in you, and everybody that's trying to ride with you isn't necessarily for you. Invite only the people who appreciate and support you unconditionally to sit at your table. Be willing to re-evaluate your circle regularly, and don't be afraid to clean house or rebuild it if necessary. When surrounded by the right people, you don't need to worry about fitting in. You can just show up as the full and real you, and the wrong people will eventually drop off.

❧ ❧

The people in my circle give more than they take.

DON'T WAIT TO BE READY

⧢

*I*t is ignorant to believe you have the next day, hour, or minute to do or say something. Tomorrow is not guaranteed, and time has no stop button. There is no genie in a bottle to grant you a magic wish, and Cinderella's clock was a fabled myth.

There is no way to return to a time before. You only get today to make the best use of your time. Be present and live in the moment. Stop holding on to the life you thought you were supposed to have and start living the life you want. Say the things that need to be said. Do the things that bring you closer to happiness. We all have an unknown expiration date.

Fulfill each day doing all the meaningful things you can and live your legacy while you're still here.

৵৵

Today I am living in the moment.

FOUR QUARTERS

*T*here are four quarters in every life. In the first quarter, we start off as a blank slate, learning as we go along. We trip, fall, and stumble a few times, dust ourselves off and conclude we've got life figured out. We think we know it all and that parents just don't understand.

In the second quarter of life, we act like we've been around for ages, and parents are out of touch or behind-the-times. We subscribe to the idea that we can do things on our own; no guidance necessary. We feel resilient, unbreakable, and ready to handle whatever life throws at us.

In the third quarter of life, we realize the universe can be merciless, and all that is golden isn't gravy.

Pushed, pulled, bruised, and damaged. We rely on our parents' wisdom to see our way through the struggles but find that eventually, we, like all of God's children, have to kneel and pray. We learn to surrender, let go and let God work his divinity in our lives. That is when we become the strongest we have ever been.

In the fourth quarter of life, we are just appreciative. We understand how blessed we are and thankful we've made it this far. Like our parents before us, it is now our turn to pass the wisdom gained onto the generations behind us.

હે જ

I have so much to give and share with the world.

SOUL'S DREAM

am who I am; it's an undisputed fact

DNA is passed down, nothing I can do about that.

The master blueprint from which all living things start

Giving my life existence, while controlling things about me, I cannot.

What my face looks like when my makeup is gone and the natural color of my skin tone.

It decides my body structure, shape, and size, and how my hair will look when left uncombed.

Inherited and passed down from generations beyond

these chemically twisted strands present irrefutable evidence of my connected bonds.

DNA may define some things about me, but it can't confine me or limit who I become.

Fate, fortune, and the future is what I'm looking to

like Jay and Bey, I'm on the run.

Heels dug in, talent working hard

Blessing and favor are in flow

I'm living my soul's dream

Never ever feelin' low.

Every morning at the start of my day

I get with the Lord and have my say

Expressing gratitude and thanks on bended knee

that DNA is not my destiny.

သြ သြ

Daily
Attitudes & Affirmations

1. When you subscribe to a life of can do, there is no room for self-doubt.

Affirmation: I am not afraid of what happens if I try. I am afraid of what happens if I don't.

2. Don't worry about things you can't change. Focus on the things you can. Start with one small thing-- correct it or get rid of it and move on to the next.

Affirmation: I make things happen.

3. If you can rise up to see another day, enjoy the sunshine, laugh about something, and make ideas happen, remember to dismiss the annoying people. You won't be missing a thing.

Affirmation: I am grateful for the people in my life who love and support me.

4. Do the things that are most important to you today just in case tomorrow decides not to show.

Affirmation: I focus my energy and give my attention to the things I value.

5. Before life gets crazy or out of control, learn to take that "S" off your chest and push back before they

push you six feet under, where the view ain't nothing but dirt.

Affirmation: My feelings and my health matter.

6. Be about the business of handling your business, and you will attract like-minded people.

Affirmation: I am never satisfied with receiving less than what I deserve, and I'm good enough to go after it.

7. If you are not getting what you need and deserve from the relationship you are in, retire their ass.

Affirmation: I am in control of changing the things that are not right in my life.

8. A rich life is filled with experiences, not things.

Affirmation: I am letting go of the life I planned to enjoy the life that is waiting for me.

9. A bad decision is not a failure; it's a lesson.

Affirmation: I invest in myself every time I learn something new or try something different.

10. Perception is a reality until someone shows you a different truth.

Affirmation: I am receptive to the opinions and ideas of others.

11. When God gives you a gift, he wraps it up in a problem. The greater the problem, the bigger the gift.

Affirmation: I am completely humbled and thankful for everything in my life.

ABOUT THE AUTHOR

RéGina Harris is a technology professional, empowerment leader, speaker, and new author with a feministic touch. She is a daily inspiration to others and known amongst friends and colleagues as a delightful, authentic, and transparent conversationalist, always encouraging and motivating.

An advocate for personal development and self-care, she uses her platform to help women navigate life's many pivotal moments with clarity and intention to become the best version of themselves.

Her love for mentoring, coaching, and public speaking was the catalyst for this uplifting literary debut. RéGina currently resides in Georgia, enjoys dancing, park hiking, and hopes to inspire women worldwide through her writing.